HO'OKELE

THE

NAVIGATOR

POEMS
BY
TIMOTHY BRANNAN

Cover Art: Original painting by Timothy Brannan

OTHER WORKS BY TIMOTHY BRANNAN

Shards of the Urn
THE END
TEARS OF ALLAH
TEACH
Adventures in Another Paradise
Manhattan Spiritual
Into the Elephant Grass
'74: A Basketball Story

© 2014 Timothy Brannan
ISBN 978-0-9820277-5-2
Published in the United States of America
Gemini Publishing LLC 2014

In honor of the ingenuity, courage and stamina of those first brave Pacific Islanders who discovered the islands we know today as the fiftieth USA state, Hawai'i

Dedicated to the memory of
Dr. Guy Owen
My mentor and friend

[February 24, 1925 – July 25, 1981]

TABLE OF CONTENTS

THE PROLOGUE: OTHER PEOPLE'S SONGS

The songs I hear all day long

are the songs of others,

other people's songs.

They seep, they sweep aside my spirit.

They leap. They creep into my chi.

With every beat I can hear it

breaking in me like the sea--

someone chanting those songs of others,

other people's songs.

Let the good seas roll and be

like a stone posing as a heart

or a salty dog unable to see

the harpoon for the harp.

There's no telemetry

by Telemecus or Tieresius, now.

Just a bonepoon in the milk-white kai[1]

where even Master Kong Zi[2] is pau[3].

He's hiding out at the Li Po[4] Basho[5]

cafe

(a witness protection program Tao[6])

as a revered and venerated Chinese

entrée.

The Li Po Basho is also world renowned

for its "Seize-the-Day" fried noodles

---

[1] Hawai`ian for sea.
[2] Venerable Chinese philosopher, Confucius.
[3] Hawai`ian for done, finished.
[4] Venerable Chinese poet.
[5] Venerable Japanese poet.
[6] Path or way that cannot be named.

and Laozi[7] Delights by the pound.
Is one of their recipes worth saving?
A song, among them, that hasn't
been sung?
Is just one of them still ringing
true when you're dangling from the
ninth rung?

The songs I hear all day long
are the songs of others,
other people's songs.

Once all have genuflected sufficiently
to all to whom they should scrape and
bow,

---

[7] Reputed author of *Tao Te Ching*.

management does, as a courtesy,

provide a fresh gelding of choice

or your favorite sacred cow

with five hooves and no voice

harnessed before yet another

debilitated plow.

The songs I hear all day long

are the songs of others,

other people's songs.

Still, the chant of Polynesian swells

carried on trade winds like leis

compels

us toward the island cays

thrice-blessed Kilo Hoku's[8] dream

foretells--

a place where sea meets mist

meets mountain meets sky.

Where canto translates into talk story,

water transubstantiates into wai,

and tangled among strings of

ukuleles,

wine dark seas transfigure into the uli

kai.[9]

---

[8] Hawai`ian for "star gazer."  The Kilo Hoku dreamed the course to be charted from the stars and passed it on to the Ho`okele, the steersman navigator.

[9] Hawai'ian for dark sea. See also fn 19 & 22.

TAO OF THE WILD WIND

TAKING YOUR CHANCES

This new wind is stale

with spores of past times,

missed touches, mountain climbs;

yet, wild at its core

with what must come before

what comes after.

Are you ready for

glances to become blows

and blows to sound like laughter?

THE ATOMS JUMPED WITH JOY

the atoms jumped with joy

when they discovered

they'd be part of a baby boy

as their first entry

into what we know as the world

but little did they realize

they'd never be able to criticize or defy

the creation of which

they had become a part.

they could only metabolize and deify

the relationship

they believed they had from the start

TAO

Is there really a way

or is that merely

the confection of

the poet and the sage?

Startled strains of

what passes for ideas

flee the embattled fields,

flushed quail

facing sawed-off

shotguns of understanding,

but,

surely, picking a path

with the point of your bayonet

through fields of

Bouncing Betties

is not the thing

that cannot be named.

POEM DRAFT

Watch where the road goes;

Catch your load flows.

What will come of it all,

no one knows or seems to recall

beyond the de-double dare

of the budding rose

and rising with the hare.

"LIFE IS BUT A BRAIN HEMORRHAGE,"

the chef countered,

without hesitation,

the argument awaited

with anticipation.

A sordid syllogism

of horror and reason

feasting on fresh greed and

greetings of the season.

A NEW POEM 2

Sides of beef

lay end to end

for miles and miles

around Song River Bend.

A fitting end to

the mending of fences

never intended.

FREE SAFETY

Your one-on-one coverage

leaves you vulnerable

through no fault of your own.

That's just the way

the play is called

from the defensive coordinator

standing in

for what cannot be called

at all.

TOSS YOUR CURDLED WORDS

Toss your curdled words, sweet loon,

at a moon that could give

a savage goddamn about you

or the tides it flings upon your shores.

It really doesn't matter, you know,

that your chatter goes nowhere

in the midnight gale

that grips the moon

with fingers of cloudy weather

shredding the sail

of sleep forever.

HOWZIT?

work

eat

sleep

urinate

defecate

that's what we reap

once we've been sown.

That's what it costs

once we've been loaned.

SHADES OF POE & FERLINGHETTI

clap trap

rat trap

scraps of cheese

in the breeze

of time

is the rhyme

the thing

or does it

simply ring

because it's struck?

RIDE THE WILD WIND

I

O to ride the wild wind

of what this thing is you value

but do not believe in,

this thing that twists you

into a double helix,

this thing that can be the end

or the beginning,

this thing that spends itself sending

or charges itself rescinding?

Is it why you call me lover, yet hover

over

endeavor and weather

detailed, dispatched, patched

into

the rue-

ful and beautiful

console

you call life?

II

O to ride the wild wind again

and then

to bend shades to blades

with raids

of rage

unequalled even by the *cul de sac* walled

against all.

III

I sure can't skewer the pure

fire

of your meteor tail thought,

but endure I can and will

all that fire

from all that ice

if it means I

can fly

the flight of perfect

love

just once

before the dove of death

takes my final breath.

HO'OKELE
THE
NAVIGATOR

WAIKIKI TWILIGHT

1

There is a time of day

in Waikiki

when the world

becomes the sea

and trade winds bear both

the promise and the curse

of yet another spring.

For pigeons, it is a time

to dip and dive in white clouds

above clanging halyards in

the Ala Wai Marina.

For the rag woman, it is a time

for tacking along the waterfront

from slip locker to slip locker,

her tattered shawl a spinnaker

around her natty head.

There is a time of day

in Waikiki

when the world

becomes the sea.

Shoures soote,

showers of blessing,

remind him, still,

of the sterility they bring.

For the recycler, it is

time for sorting and breaking

the day's bottles, unaware

that he creates Dvořák

in the dusk of ages:

crashing beer bottles

of ages past;

crunching whiskey jugs

of present ages;

crack and tingle of champagne

magnum future ages

and ages snapping back again.

For the navigator, Ho'okele,

it is a time to contemplate

the deeds and lack of them

that hang about his neck

with the weight of `ilima and maile

leis.[10]

There is a time of day

in Waikiki

when the world

becomes the sea.

2

A mole

by any other name

---

[10] Maile, a fragrant vine in Hawai'i's upland forests, may be the oldest and most favored lei material used by early Hawaiians. Maile was the lei of all the people and was associated with worship of the gods, particularly of Laka, the goddess of dance. The lei was given in olden times as a peace offering on the field of battle, maile today is frequently chosen for graduations and is used in ceremonies to bless new buildings. The *'ilima* lei lasts only the day or the evening. It's worth lies in giving, not in the amount of time it lasts.

would stealth and crash

as sweet.

Yet this mole

has not yet bored to

the roots of his virus.

He still calculates

the number of quarters

he must work before

retirement sets in.

Or he might contemplate

the curve of

the Dow Jones Average

as if it were

the Blue Girl of his youth

on a night of the full moon

when the trades caressed

to the point of stinging pleasure—

better than lips,

tongue,

teeth.

Rain dangles in the air

but no longer falls

in showers of blessing

onto the rhinestone spires

of Waikiki.

The mole is finally done.

Like Keats and Shelley under Coleridge's

dome,

he awakes with nightmares

at every turn.

The truth that will burn

free,

the beauty of the urn

tree.

The ghosts that churn and haunt.

The riddles that daunt

he;

The path that he won't

see.

Driven by necessity,

a finger squeezes

the trigger

of his brain.

3

The Aloha's broken mast lies lashed

to the storm-shattered starboard deck.

Her engine, silent.

Her cabin portals, dark.

The moon is whole and golden

fractured only by black clouds.

Her song, a shriek in the night,

the Blue Girl's chant takes flight

and drives a marlin spike

into his already-bleeding heart.

Hair and fingernails

are all that remain of her ardore,

Blue Girl of his youth.

Her passion was the lagoon where

his daydreams spawned.

Her commune, his safe harbor.

4

There is a time of day

in Waikiki

when the world

becomes the sea.

A time when

daydreams and nightmares

erupt on equal terms

in the volcanoes of

imagination.

From the ash and lava flow

of this twilight,

the beginning and the end

merge.

No further point

of reference exists.

Yet, Ho'okele steers

the refitted Aloha onward.

No shadow. No shade.

No sun on his back.

Just the way forward

and the way back again.

ON THE TENTH DAY AFTER THE LAST FULL MOON: THE APOCALYPSE[11]

No song of the legend of Rata's Canoe[12]

had yet been sung when a shard from

a splintered tree became an oar, too,

in the hands of a drowning dawn.

---

[11] "Hawaiians as Navigators and Seamen," Samuel Wilder King, *34th Annual Report of the Hawaiian Historical Society*, 1925, 11-14. General reference throughout this poem.

[12] Polynesian legend in which King Rata of Tahiti goes on his mission for the dead. During the voyage, he faces and vanquishes seven foes of the deep: Pu'a-tu-tahi-Coral-rock-standing-alone; Ahifa-tu-moana-Sea-serpent; 'Are-mata-roroa-Long wave; 'Are-mata-popoto-Short wave; Pahua-nui-api-taa-i-te-ra'i-Giant Clam that opens against the sky; Anae-moe-oho-Shoal of monsters; Tupe-io-ahu-Beast of heated flesh; 'Otu'u-ha'a-mana-a-Ta'aroa-Stork-exalted by Ta'aroa.

The first germ is the first germ

though not necessarily the best,

although it anticipated

shared experience and the test,

as the ancient master Ho`okele navigated

the Chosen toward Kilo Hoku's dream.

Across the endless ocean,

beyond the limitless sea

looms the untouchable illusion,

giant-clam-opening-at-the-horizon.

With the earliest Marqueses migration

over two thousand years ago,

voyagers began habitation

of every island and atoll.

They set sail in outrigger canoes

for the unreachable zone,

toward pillars of the rising sun taboos

near the heart of the great unknown.

Remote as the coral heads they lived on,

they yearned to know what lay beyond

the untouchable illusion,

giant-clam-opening-at-the-horizon.

The homeland of those kanaka maoli[13]

who first sailed to the islands over the

rainbow sea

were being invaded by philosophies,

contrary to the teachings they believed.

With war between islands a certainty

[13] Native Hawaiian.

soon to engulf even their community,

the elders of the village sought unity

as they contemplated impending slavery.

Across the endless ocean,

beyond the limitless sea

looms the untouchable illusion,

giant-clam-opening-at-the-horizon.

Kilo Hoku, the eminent seer,

made his vision atoll-water clear:

"I ventured in my spirit form,

guided by mothers of the ancestral realm,

through the last black night of the new moon.

They showed me a lei of new islands beyond

sun pillars and giant-clam-opening-at-the-horizon.

Now, the council, must determine who will
go

To resettle in that far archipelago."

Across the endless ocean,
beyond the limitless sea
looms the untouchable illusion,
giant-clam-opening-at-the-horizon.

On the tenth day after the last full moon,
villagers built fires along the shore
and loaded provisions onto canoes
numbering four.[14]

---

[14] The following material comes from an internet
publication by Chad Baybayan:
The land and sea provided Hawaiians with everything they

Voyagers selected

by family traits and skills.

Tools crafted.

Plants cultivated.

Animals fatted.

Fear subjugated.

The crew left their families

and boarded the created.

---

needed to sustain themselves. During the early stages of a voyage, the seamen ate fresh foods from their homeland. After those initial days at sea, nourishment consisted primarily of dried and fermented foods prepared by their families before their trip began. Fishing along the way supplemented food the voyagers brought with them. The Polynesians had to be excellent horticulturist also if they expected to survive once they got to land. Plants were transported as slips, cuttings, tubers and seedlings.

The traditional diet included plant food such as 'ulu (breadfruit); niu (coconut, meat and drink); uhi (yam); 'uala (sweet potato); mai'a (banana); kalo (taro); kukui (candlenut); ko (sugar cane); hala (pandanus flour, paste) and animal food like i'a (fish, dried and fresh); pua'a (pig); moa (chicken); 'ilio (dog).

Elders blessed the four vessels
when the tide was at its height
and launched them with tears of sadness
into the woeful night.

.

Across the endless ocean,
beyond the limitless sea
looms the untouchable illusion,
giant-clam-opening-at-the-horizon.

The sea-faring canoes talked
with drums, flags, and conchs.
Ho`okele navigated by Kilo Huko's
dream maps of the rising and setting stars
and the gift of his father's knowledge
and of all the Wayfinders before.

Between the rising and setting sun

he read wave swells to keep his course.

At night, he read the stars until

clouds obscured the sky,

when, once more, the ocean swells

were all on which he could rely.

Across the endless ocean,

beyond the limitless sea

looms the untouchable illusion,

giant-clam-opening-at-the-horizon.

The course of the sailing fleet was straight

for a dark shadow suddenly erasing the

horizon.

Hands strained.

Arms bulged.

The voyagers fought for control

of the large steering blades and sails

when the lei-strewn winds howled

and the limitless sea swept their hulls.

Bailers furiously emptied the canoes

as they touched the untouchable illusion,

and sailed through the heart of

giant-clam-opening-at-the-horizon.

As suddenly, the kai was calm.

Sea bird signs,

varied coloration in the clouds,

debris floating on the ocean waters,

and a particular scent in the air

all hinted at land being near.

Drums pounded,

Conchs bellowed,

The voyagers chanted and cheered.

Across the endless ocean,

beyond the limitless sea

no longer looms the untouchable illusion,

giant-clam-opening-at-the-horizon.

The canoes encircled the first island

seeking some safe landing.

The waters along the reefs and shoreline

sparkled

with schools of darting silver fish.

Water cascaded down cliffs carved in

lush mountains of velvet green

that would soon caress the plants from home.

Landfall came in the islands of the rainbows as promised in Kilo Hoku's dream.[15]

---

[15] From Voyaging into New Horizons, E. Kalani Flores.

HO`OKELE, THE STEERSMAN

The cool Pacific sprayed

Over Aloha's dipping bow

Making Ho`okele wonder how

He could have ever strayed.

He chanted "'U'u! U'u! U'u!"[16]

Hauling in the lines like Wayfinders'

knowledge,

he hoisted the sloop's mainsail into

the gusts and lulls of the carnage

---

[16] Hawai`ian sailing canoe term for "Haul on the lines" or "Pull on the lines."

inherent in the winds of trade.

"Wehe ka pe'a!"[17]

He opened the sail.

The past was behind him now--

Kaua`i and Ni`ihau.

"Ho`omalo!"[18]

He tied the lines taut.

Before him, in the uli,[19]

beyond his lantern's glow,

the future that he sought

spread before him like the flow

---

[17] Hawai`ian sailing canoe term for "Open the sail."

[18] Hawai`ian sailing canoe term for " make taut, as a cord or a sail."

[19] Hawai`ian for "Any dark color including the deep blue of the sea, the ordinary green of vegetation, and the dark of black clouds; the black-and-blue of a bruise. Some writers avoid this word because connotations of evil and misfortune are associated with darkness. Also uli uli and kai uli, the deep sea. The name of the goddess of sorcery, said to have come from Kahiki.

of the caressing sea.

"Poholua!"[20]

The sail billowed

toward Maui, Molaka`i, Lana`i,

The Big Island, and

the new lava flowing island Lo`ihi.

Ho`okele, the steersman,

was, once again, chasing

Kilo Hoku's star maps

across the uli kai,[21]

while Aloha groaned beneath him

from the force of the swells

pounding against her hull

---

[20] Hawai`ian sailing canoe term for " billow out, as sails."
[21] See fn 19 above and 22 below.

like the beat of an ancient anthem.

The cool Pacific sprayed

Over Aloha's rising bow

Making Ho`okele wonder how

He could have ever strayed.

IN A FALSE LIGHT

It was the first night out that he introverted

and first diverted

to the false light of a false dawn.

While he waited for the false alarm,

watering and feeding the false prawns,

a spiny lobster ate through him

with the voracity of a moray eel

and the ease of a laser beam,

forever calling itself maturity.

But Odysseus called himself no-man

when he escaped the cave of

the Cyclops he had blinded with

the fire-tempered spear

of his ingenuity.
Didn't he?

In the false light of that first night,
he became aware,
that being gutted by a crayfish
demanding to be called a lobster
wasn't really maturity at all.
It was merely fear.

HE COULD VIEW FROM THE CROW'S NEST OF TRUTH

He could view

From the crow's nest

All that had ever been true

About the courses he had pressed

And the courses he had not

As well, of course, as the rest

He had not even thought.

With an engine wheeze

And the smell of a storm

Filling the brisk sea breeze

Of an, otherwise, warm

And perfect sailing day,

Ho`okele understood, for these

Views, he might have to pay.

GORGEOUS GARGOYLE

E lauhoe mai na wa'a; i ke ka, i ka hoe;
i ka hoe, i ke ka;
pae aku i ka 'aina.

[Translation: "Paddle together, bail, paddle; paddle, bail; paddle towards the land." On inter-island trips, heavy seas often washed over the canoe. At these times, the two most important functions of the crew were to paddle and to bail. Some would be constantly bailing. Others would paddle together on command to reach their destination in the shortest time.]

Second night out

erupting clouds blocked

the near full moon and the stars

from Ho`okele's view.

He chanted into the storm:

" E lauhoe mai na wa'a;

i ke ka, i ka hoe;

i ka hoe, i ke ka;

pae aku i ka 'aina"

from the old ways.

Paddle together, bail, paddle;

paddle, bail;

paddle towards the land.

Alone and overwhelmed,

he lashed himself to the wheel

as white-capped lava swelled

above Aloha's mast

and swept across her decks

as if they were not occupying

the same time and space.

Gorgeous gargoyle

come close so that I may see.

The death in your eyes

is no Sargasso to me.

And, he chanted with breath

Of the storm itself,

" E lauhoe mai na wa'a;

i ke ka, i ka hoe;

i ka hoe, i ke ka;

pae aku i ka 'aina"

from the old ways.

DISMASTED AND ADRIFT

Pacific swells no longer

shoved at the guts

of the antique sloop.

Dismasted and adrift,

Aloha's Kapane Ho`okele

was far too weak to release

himself from the lines

that still lashed him

to the Captain's wheel.

The sea was glass.

Aloha's mast

floated just off the bow.

Dehydrated and

starving,

he imagined

hoisting

the splintered spar from the ocean

and jamming it into place.

The sea was glass.

Aloha's mast

floated just off the bow.

He imagined a strong wind

filling the sloop's sails.

But all the flat kai

would provide

was a water spout to port

that Ho`okele swore

was his Blue Girl

or Uli

goddess of sorcery

borne up by the beetle nut sea

to remind him of his mortality.

The sea was glass.

Aloha's mast

floated just off the bow.

E Uli e,

e Uli nana pono,

e Uli nana hewa,

e Uli I uka,

e Uli I kai.[22]

The fetal beginning

and the fatal cliffs of darkness

at the end.

---

[22] Uli: the Hawai`ian goddess of sorcery. The chant: O Uli, O Uli observe good, O Uli observe evil, O Uli inland, O Uli seaward.

UPON REALIZING THAT AN AUTOMATIC REFLEX IS NOT AUTOMATIC AFTER ALL

Sometimes, now, he forgets how to breathe.

He writhes and wheezes in the

memory of maile and `ilima heavy mists

saturating his home, the Valley of the

Temples.

Breathing isn't an automatic reflex after all,

even in a sacred place.

Or, so it seems in his memories

on his darkest night.

He would grieve
in the manner of his ancestors
for the loss of his only friend,
The star-gazer, Kilo Hoku.
That had been his name in youth.
Dead—more than thirty years dead now—
Kilo Hoku and their art,
both together and apart.
But he cannot penetrate
the petroglyphs of the kapuna,[23]
so how can he know the manner
of their mourning
or the color of their night?

[23] An elder in the Hawai`ian culture.

Instead, he did not participate

even though he knew it

to be axiomatic that the rate

of self-defeat increases

exponentially with

every failure to engage.

Pele damn the gun and the bow.

Give him the pahoa, [24]

fire-tempered and so

perfectly intimate that

he knew which way to go

and which way not.

---

[24] An ancient traditional knife made by and used by practitioners of the Hawai`ian martial art Lua.

Which way was grief

and which way was gut.

MASKS OF THE
HAWAI`IAN MOON

The full blood moon and gale force

trades

Lasered and sheared dynamic

shades

From banks of cumulous nimbus clay

Erupting across the uli-uli day

As if they were squeezed by

menehune[25] elves

From the Ko`olau mountains

---

[25] Hawai`ian elves or leprechans or some say an ancient race that settled the islands long before the Hawai`ians landed. Whatever their origin, they were legendary as engineers and builders, particularly of walls and water ditches which, as legend has it, they would construct overnight.

themselves.

Three headless maids and a

drowning man

Drifted from port to starboard,

Seeking, of all things, hope in a can

And some semblance of safe harbor,

While the relentless

Cccccccccccccccccccccccrack

Of frantic firing

Settled like a morning fog

Over the songs of headless

Ssssssssssssssssssssssssssirenes.

"Halt in the name of the

cccccccccccccccccccccccrew!"

Chanted the primal

Sssssssssssssssssssssssssssstew

As the ho`okele's head went under

For the final time or two.

"A will of steel

Will not heal

A wound from steel,"

Ho`okele chanted even though he

was aware

That his words might not be worthy.

They were not, after all, the kapuna's

fare,

Rather his own mêlées hurtling toward the

petroglyph flurry—

Meteors dispersing into the same

moon-and-wind-shorn

storm from which they were born.

Among wind sheared clouds of the
less-than-conscious,
Planes of thought frolic, then plummet
on top of us
Like Spinner Dolphins off the
starboard bow
Toward the granite cliffs of reason
Or the lava flow of treason somehow,
Depending upon the tilt of the
airplane's wings
When the trade winds howl and the
angel sings.

EPILOGUE:
EMI MAI KA LA!

Chant: " 'Alu na pe'a! Pani ka pe'a!
Emi mai ka la!"

'Alu na pe'a! Ease the sheets,
and let the wind free.
Pani ka pe'a! Close the sail.
Emi mai ka la! Lower the sail.

The chant no longer seemed to apply
near the end of the fifth day of his
ordeal
when Ho`okele finally motored the

frail

and dismasted Aloha into her slip at

the Ala Wai.

Chant: " 'Alu na pe'a! Pani ka pe'a! Emi mai
ka la!"

THE
"LAKE ISLE" GAFFER

What is this, then,

that still gaffs the heart?

Imagine the mast upright,

full sail ho'omalo in the teeth

of the trades.

It has been subjected to so much

idolatry yet stands alone

and apart from all others—

the single fang in an otherwise toothless

mouth.

Is it really "Lake Isle" and then you're free?

Otherwise, you're pau?

ABOUT THE AUTHOR

Timothy Brannan is a poet, novelist, composer, and painter born in Raleigh, North Carolina. He holds a Bachelor of Arts in English and Philosophy and a Master of Arts in Literature and Writing from NC State University. Both as an undergraduate and a graduate student he was mentored by the late Dr. Guy Owen (*Ballad of the Flim-Flam Man, Journey for Joedel, The White Stallion and Other Poems*) and submitted the first creative writing Master's thesis ever accepted at NC State University nearly thirty years before the university established an official MFA program. He later earned a Juris Doctor from Florida State University.

Timothy worked more than five years on Oahu as a chief of staff, legal counsel, and political consultant where he was continually exposed to the great and heroic history of the Pacific Island canoe sailors, the inspiration for *Ho'okele The Navigator*.

www.ingramcontent.com/pod-product-compliance
Lightning Source LLC
Chambersburg PA
CBHW021141020426
42331CB00005B/859